Contents

What is a rainforest?

Rainforests grow in hot and wet places.

Rainforests have many trees.

Living in the

Rainforest

Rebecca Rissman

Raintree is an imprint of Capstone Global Library Limited, a company incorporated in England and Wales having its registered office at 7 Pilgrim Street, London, EC4V 6LB – Registered company number: 6695582

www.raintreepublishers.co.uk
myorders@raintreepublishers.co.uk

Text © Capstone Global Library Limited 2014
First published in hardback in 2014
Paperback edition first published in 2015
The moral rights of the proprietor have been asserted.

Edited by Daniel Nunn, Rebecca Rissman, and Catherine Veitch
Designed by Cynthia Della-Rovere
Picture research by Tracy Cummins
Production by Sophia Argyris
Originated by Capstone Global Library Ltd
Printed and bound in China by Leo Paper Products Ltd

ISBN 978 1 406 26590 3 (hardback)
17 16 15 14 13
10 9 8 7 6 5 4 3 2 1

ISBN 978 1 406 26597 2 (paperback)
18 17 16 15 14
10 9 8 7 6 5 4 3 2 1

British Library Cataloguing in Publication Data
A full catalogue record for this book is available from the British Library.

Acknowledgements
We would like to thank the following for permission to reproduce photographs: Getty Images pp. 8 (© Jens Kuhfs), 17 (© Rob Blakers); istockphoto pp. 1, 13 (© Anand Sharma), 15 (© 4FR); Shutterstock pp. 4 (© Stephane Bidouze), 6, 23a (© Dr. Morley Read), 7 (© Uryadnikov Sergey), 9 (© Nigel Smith), 10 (© Janne Hämäläinen), 11 (© Vitaly Titov & Maria Sidelnikova), 12 (© ehtesham), 14, 23b (© Christopher Meder), 16 (© Valery Shanin), 18 (© Jason Mintzer), 19 (© formiktopus), 20 (© Jerry Dupree), 22 (© Igor S.), 23c (© Galyna Andrushko); Superstock pp. 5 (© Minden Pictures).

Front cover photograph of Jaguar reproduced with permission of Superstock (© Minden Pictures).

We would like to thank Michael Bright and Diana Bentley for their invaluable help in the preparation of this book.

Every effort has been made to contact copyright holders of material reproduced in this book. Any omissions will be rectified in subsequent printings if notice is given to the publisher.

Some words are in bold, **like this**.
You can find them in the glossary on page 23.

Different types of plants and animals live in rainforests.

There are **non-living** things in rainforests, too.

What are living things?

Living things are alive. Living things need air and **sunlight**. Living things move on their own.

Living things need food and water.

Living things grow and change.

What are non-living things?

Non-living things are not alive. Non-living things do not need air and **sunlight**.

Non-living things do not need food or water.

non-living

non-living

Non-living things do not move on their own.

Non-living things do not grow and change on their own.

Is a river living or non-living?

A river does not need food.

A river does not grow on its own.

A river does not need air or **sunlight**.

A river is **non-living**.

Is a bird living or non-living?

A bird needs food and water.

A bird moves on its own.

A bird grows and changes.

A bird needs air and **sunlight**.

A bird is **living**.

Is a tree living or non-living?

A tree grows and changes.

A tree needs air and **sunlight**.

A tree moves on its own towards the sun.

A tree needs water.

A tree is **living**.

Is soil living or non-living?

Soil does not move on its own.

Soil does not need food or water.

Soil does not grow on its own.

Soil does not need air or **sunlight**.

Soil is **non-living**.

Is a frog living or non-living?

A frog grows and changes.

A frog needs air and **sunlight**.

A frog needs food and water.

A frog moves on its own.

A frog is **living**.

Is a rock living or non-living?

A rock does not move on its own.

A rock does not need food or water.

A rock does not grow on its own.

A rock does not need air or **sunlight**.

A rock is **non-living**.

What do you think?

Is this butterfly **living** or **non-living**?

Glossary

living alive. Living things need food and water. They breathe and move on their own. They grow and change.

non-living not alive. Non-living things do not need food or water. They do not move on their own. They do not grow and change on their own.

sunlight light from the sun

Find out more

Websites

Click through these images of living and non-living things, then take a quiz!
www.bbc.co.uk/schools/scienceclips/ages/5_6/ourselves.shtml

Check out this site to learn more about what living things need.
www.kidsbiology.com/biology_basics/needs_living_things/living_things_have_needs1.php

Go to this site and try to spot all the living things in the park!
www.sciencekids.co.nz/gamesactivities/plantsanimals.html

Books

A Rainforest Habitat (Introducing Habitats), Molly Aloian and Bobbie Kalman (Crabtree, 2006)

Living and Nonliving, Carol K. Lindeen (Capstone Press, 2008)

Rainforest Animals (Animals in Their Habitats), Francine Galko (Raintree, 2002)

Index